A New True Book

WHITE-TAILED DEER

By Joan Kalbacken

CHILDRENS PRESS®

CHICAGO

Fawn of a white-tailed deer

PHOTO CREDITS

© Cameramann International, Ltd.—13 (right)

© Alan D. Carey—Cover

© Alan & Sandy Carey—8 (top left, center left, bottom right), 14 (bottom right), 31 (right), 41 (right), 43, 44

Department of Natural Resources, Sandhill-Meadow Valley Work Unit—© John Kubisiak, 40 (right)

H. Armstrong Roberts—© M. Barrett, 2; © T. Dietrich, 15 (right); © W. Metzen, 28, 30

© Jerry Hennen—8 (top right), 11, 19 (bottom right)

North Wind Picture Archives—10, 13 (left)

Photri—4, 7, 12, 14 (bottom left), 19 (top right), 22, 32, 41 (left), 42, 45; © B. Kulik, 17 (right); © Leonard Lee Rue III, 25 (right); © Glen Jackson, 33 (right)

Root Resources—© Jim Nachel, 16 (right); © Anthony Mercierca, 36 (bottom right)

SuperStock International, Inc.—© Tom Rosenthal, 23 (right); © Leonard Lee Rue III, 24, 25 (left)

TSW-CLICK/Chicago—© Leonard Lee Rue III, 8 (bottom left), 15 (left), 19 (top left), 20 (right), 36 (top left & right, bottom right)

Visuals Unlimited—© Leonard Lee Rue III, 5; © Ron Spomer, 8 (center right), 31 (left); © William J. Weber, 14 (top), 16 (left), 21, 23 (left), 26; © W.A. Banaszewski, 17 (left), 19 (bottom left), 29, 33 (left); © Tom Edwards, 20 (left); © Dick Thomas, 34, 40 (left); © Frank L. Lambrecht, 35 (left); © Dee Culleny, 35 (right); © R. Calentine, 39 (left); © Fred Marsik, 39 (right)

Cover: White-tailed buck

Library of Congress Cataloging-in-Publication Data

Kalbacken, Joan.
  White-tailed deer / by Joan Kalbacken.
    p.   cm. — (A New true book)
  Includes index.
  Summary: Describes the physical characteristics, habits, and habitat of the whitetail, or Virginia, deer. Also discusses some of the problems these animals face.
  ISBN 0-516-01138-3
  1. White-tailed deer—Juvenile literature.
[1. White-tailed deer. 2. Deer.] I. Title.
QL737.U55K35 1992
599.73'57—dc20   91-35277
                          CIP
                          AC

TABLE OF CONTENTS

A POPULAR ANIMAL

Deer raising its white
tail, like a flag, as it runs

White-tailed deer are popular. In five states—Illinois, Mississippi, New Hampshire, Pennsylvania, and South Carolina—schoolchildren voted to make the white-tailed deer their state animal.

The white-tailed deer is named for the pure white underside of its tail. It flips its tail up when it runs.

In Wisconsin, the white-tailed deer
is the state's wildlife animal.

Sometimes people call this deer the Virginia deer. The English settlers first saw the white-tailed deer in the Virginia Colony. Often, people just call this deer the whitetail.

White-tailed deer may have arrived in North America from Asia some 25 million years ago.

Whitetails are found in every state except Hawaii.

A group of white-tailed deer. Only the males have antlers.

They live mostly in the eastern, midwestern, and southern states. They are also found in Mexico and Canada. Very few deer are found in high mountain regions.

7

Some North American deer (clockwise from top left): bull moose, cow moose with calf, mule deer, male elk, cow elk with calf, and caribou

WHITETAIL RELATIVES

   North America has five
major kinds of deer. They
are whitetails, mule deer,
caribou, elk, and moose.
At 6 feet (1.8 meters), the
moose is the largest. A big
adult male whitetail is 3 ½ feet
(1.1 meters) high and weighs
200 pounds (91 kilograms).
The whitetail is fast. Its
running speed is between
30 and 40 miles (48 and 64
kilometers) per hour.

FOOD AND CLOTHING FROM DEER

The Native Americans hunted deer with bows and arrows.

The white-tailed deer was the Native Americans' favorite wild animal. They hunted whitetails for food and clothing. Deer meat, called venison, is tasty, fat-free, and easy to prepare.

Deerskins make good clothing. They are soft, even after being soaked in water. Buffalo, elk, and bear skins are not.

Native Americans wearing buckskin clothing

The male deer is called
a buck. Native Americans
wore clothing made from
buckskins because they
were tough and long-
wearing.   11

White-tailed deer like to live in woodlands. The males
are called bucks; the females are called does.

The female deer is
called a doe. Does are
smaller than bucks. Native
American women chewed
doeskins to make them
very soft for children's
clothes.

Trading with the European settlers (left). A Native American woman makes clothing from deerskins.

Native Americans traded buckskins for things they needed from the settlers. The skins were called "bucks." Even today, the American dollar is often called a "buck."

13

FOOD AND WATER FOR DEER

White-tailed deer feed in small fields near wooded areas. They eat tender grasses, leaves, and the twigs of shrubs and trees.

Whitetails eat grasses and the twigs of trees.
The deer at bottom right is feasting on fallen apples.

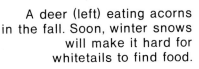
A deer (left) eating acorns in the fall. Soon, winter snows will make it hard for whitetails to find food.

They eat the acorns that fall from oak trees in autumn. They also enjoy apples. Their food supply depends on the summer and winter weather. Dry summers and deep snowy winters make it difficult for deer to find food.

15

Deer like the grassy plants
that grow in lakes and streams.
They will wade into icy water
to drink.

Besides a good food
supply, the deer need
water. Whitetails live near
lakes, rivers, and creeks.
They also drink from cattle
water tanks or lick snow in
winter. In warm weather,
an adult deer drinks 2 to 3

quarts (1.9 to 2.8 liters) of
water each day. It drinks
twice that much in winter.

Woods provide shelter
and hiding places for deer.
During cold weather
whitetails seek deep snow
cover to keep warm. In
warm weather they look
for shade to stay cool.

A fawn hides in leafy woodland (left). A buck (right)
manages to keep warm in deep winter snow.

THE LIFE OF THE BUCK

Bucks are larger and stronger than does. Bucks live by themselves while their antlers grow. With his hard hooves, a buck scratches special places in the woods. These "scrapes" are part of his territory.

Bucks shed their antlers in winter and grow a new set each spring. In five months or less, a buck can grow huge antlers.

Antlers are like special bones that grow rapidly.

At first antlers are soft.
A fuzzy covering called
velvet protects the antlers
as they grow.

Young bucks grow small
antlers. Older bucks have
antlers with six to eight

The growth of antlers: Antlers grow from these knoblike bones
on the skull (top left). New antlers growing (top right). Antlers
covered with velvet (bottom right). Close-up of velvet (bottom left).

The antlers of some older bucks grow long and form many branches.

points called tines. If the food supply has been good, bucks grow larger antlers. Some antlers may have a dozen or more tines. However, the oldest deer do not always grow the largest antlers.

MATING

A buck shedding the velvet from his antlers

Before mating season begins, the buck rubs the velvet coating from his antlers. He polishes his antlers on branches of small trees. Sharp, hard antlers help the buck. He uses his antlers to defend himself and protect his territory. Sometimes he uses his sharp hooves, too.

The mating time, or "rut," begins in October. During "rutting" season, bucks often fight each other. They sometimes lock their antlers together when fighting.

Fawns may stay with their
mother for over a year.

THE FAWNS

Fawns are usually born
in April or May. The doe
hides in a thick brushy
area when she gives birth.
She often has twins.

Newborn fawns weigh
from 5 to 7 pounds (2 to 3
kilograms). Fawns can

23

A fawn can stand and walk right after it is born.

stand and walk right after
they are born. Their
spotted and odorless
bodies help them hide.
Their spotted coats change
to brown with specks of
gray and black by the
time they are four months
old.

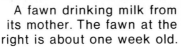
A fawn drinking milk from its mother. The fawn at the right is about one week old.

White-tailed deer are mammals. Fawns drink milk from their mothers. They grow strong quickly. A week-old fawn can run faster than a human. The doe teaches her fawns to stay very still. They are taught to be alert to danger.

25

A deer stops in the middle of a drink to listen for danger.

SHARP SENSES

The senses of whitetails
are very sharp. They
communicate with other
deer by moving their tails,
bodies, and ears. Raised
tails or erect ears tell
others to be careful. A

front-foot stomp is a warning of danger nearby.

Fawns sometimes bleat like a lamb when they want their mother. Does talk to their fawns in a high-pitched tone. Their calls are so high that humans cannot hear them. Large bucks grunt or snort when in trouble.

Deer have a keen sense of smell. They can smell a human being from a

distance of 100 feet (30.4 meters). Any odor stays in the deer's memory.

White-tailed deer have a gland between their hooves that makes an odor. The

The gland that produces the odor is in this opening in the deer's hooves.

strong smell is left on the ground when the deer walks. This odor helps deer track one another.

Whitetails hear sounds at great distances. Their sense of hearing is much better than that of humans. They know the sounds that mean possible danger.

Any unusual noise frightens the whitetails. They become jittery and may flee. White-tailed deer detect movement much quicker

White-tailed deer stay together in small groups.

Whitetails are excellent jumpers.
Fences do not stop them.

than humans. Their eyesight
is excellent. At seeing a
sudden strange movement,
a deer may leap an 8-foot
(2.4-meter) fence. In one
single jump a deer can
cover 20 feet (6 meters).
However, deer cannot see
colors as well as humans.

WHITETAILS AND PEOPLE

Many deer die each year. In deep snow some deer cannot move enough to find food, and they may starve. Some deer die each year from pneumonia and other diseases.

Starving deer in winter snow

This fawn was injured by
a dog. Deer-crossing signs
let drivers know that deer
trails cross the road.

Predators kill a number of
deer for food.

Whitetails often get into
trouble when they wander
into towns or get too close
to highways. Many
thousands of deer are
killed on the highways
each year.

33

In one year, more than 38,000 deer were killed
by automobiles in a midwestern state.

Deer need three things
to survive: food, water, and
places to hide. In the past,
the use of land for housing,
industry, and farming took
away deer habitats.

But in recent years,
deer have reclaimed some

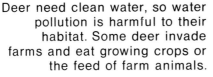
Deer need clean water, so water pollution is harmful to their habitat. Some deer invade farms and eat growing crops or the feed of farm animals.

of these areas. They are abundant in farm country and in forest preserves near cities. Sometimes they wander into suburban areas, where they may eat valuable young trees and shrubs.

Deer predators (clockwise from top left): Bobcat, cougar, bear, and wolf

PREDATORS

Whitetails are food for
many carnivorous, or meat-
eating, animals. Cougars,
wolves, bobcats, coyotes,
bears, and even dogs
hunt deer. But the greatest
predators are people.

In the 1600s and 1700s, there were millions of whitetails in North America. But by the end of the 1800s, there were less than 800,000 left. Game preserves were set up to protect the deer. In some places, deer hunting was banned. Today, there are more than 14 million deer in the United States, and hunting seasons have been established in every state to keep deer numbers in balance with their habitat.

SCIENTISTS ARE HELPING THE WHITETAILS

The white-tailed deer sometimes carry tiny ticks in their fur. The ticks do not harm the deer, but they carry a bacteria that can cause illness in other forms of life.

When the ticks leave the deer, they feed on other animals and people. The ticks are blood-suckers that inject the bacteria as

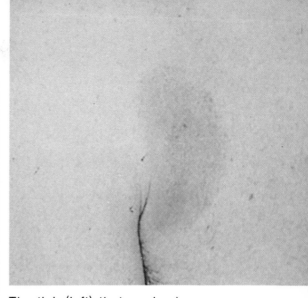

The tick (left) that carries Lyme disease is shown here many times its real size. Usually, the first sign of infection is a rash that spreads from the tick bite.

they feed. The bacteria cause Lyme disease, which can be very painful.

Scientists are searching for ways to prevent Lyme disease.

Scientists measure antlers and check deer trails
to help keep track of the size and numbers of deer.

At deer-checking stations, biologists examine thousands of deer. They record the weight, age, and measurements of the deer. The does and bucks are counted. The deer are checked for size and health.

Biologists help the states decide on hunting regulations. Some years the hunting season is short. Sometimes only bucks may be killed.

Game wardens enforce hunting regulations. They prevent people from killing

Regulated hunting helps control deer populations so that fewer deer will damage farmers' crops or wander onto highways to be killed by cars.

deer illegally during the
hunting season and from
hunting outside the season.
White-tailed deer are
strong animals. They are
able to survive many
hardships. However, they
do not have a very long
life. Most deer live less

than two years. Very few
live to be more than ten
years old.

Wildlife experts are
helping the white-tailed deer.
They are protecting their
feeding grounds and saving
the white-tailed deer for
future generations to enjoy.

WORDS YOU SHOULD KNOW

abundant (uh • BUN • dent) — occurring in great numbers; plentiful

acorn (AY • korn) — the nutlike fruit of the oak tree

alert (uh • LERT) — watchful; aware

antlers (ANT • lerz) — a bony, hornlike growth on the head of an animal such as a white-tailed deer or moose

bacteria (bak • TIR • ee • ah) — tiny living things that can be seen only with a microscope; some bacteria cause illness

banned (BAND) — not allowed; made illegal

biologist (by • AH • luh • jist) — a scientist who studies living things

caribou (KAIR • ih • boo) — a large deer that lives in the far north

carnivorous (car • NIH • ver • iss) — meat-eating

colony (KAH • luh • nee) — a settlement of people who have come from another country

communicate (kuh • MYOO • nih • kait) — to pass information back and forth

detect (dih • TEKT) — to become aware of; to find

erect (ih • REKT) — standing upright

game preserve (GAIM prih • ZERV) — a place set aside to protect an animal that is in danger from humans

game warden (GAIM WAR • din) — an official who watches to see that hunters obey the laws

generation (jen • er • RAY • shun) — all the people who are about the same age and who live at the same time

gland (GLAND) — a special body part that makes things that the body can use or give off

habitat (HAB • ih • tat) — home; the place where an animal usually lives

hardship (HARD • ship) — difficult living conditions

hooves (HOOVZ) — the horny feet of some animals such as cows and deer

Lyme disease (LYM dih •ZEEZ) —a disease of humans caused by the ticks that are carried by deer

mammal (MAM • il) —one of a group of warm-blooded animals that have hair and nurse their young with milk

odorless (OH • der • less) —having no smell

pneumonia (nih • MOAN • ya) —a disease of the lungs

predator (PREH • dih • ter) —one who hunts and kills animals

reclaim (REE •KLAIM) —to take back

regulation (reg • yoo • LAY • shun) —a rule; a law

settlers (SET • lerz) —people who make their homes in a new country

territory (TAIR • ih • tor • ee) —an area with definite boundaries that an animal lives in

tick (TIK) —a small animal that is related to spiders

tines (TYNZ) —points; blades

valuable (VAL • yu • uh • bul) —costing much money

venison (VEN • ih • sun) —deer meat

INDEX

About the Author

Joan Formell Kalbacken earned a BA in Education from the University of Wisconsin, Madison. After graduate work at Coe College, Iowa, and the University of Toulouse, France, she received an MA from Illinois State University, Normal, Illinois. She was a secondary school teacher in Beloit, Wisconsin, and Pekin and Normal, Illinois. She taught French and mathematics for twenty-nine years, and she also served as foreign language supervisor in Normal. She received the award for excellence in Illinois' program, "Those Who Excel."

She is past state president of the Delta Kappa Gamma Society International and a member of Pi Delta Phi, Kappa Delta Pi, AAUW, and Phi Delta Kappa.